ISBN

978-1-965005-90-3

Page Intentionally Left Blank

A Harmonic Minor Scale Studies
La Menor Armoníca

Practice each hand seperately first and then together.

Carlos Maldonado

1

Whole Notes

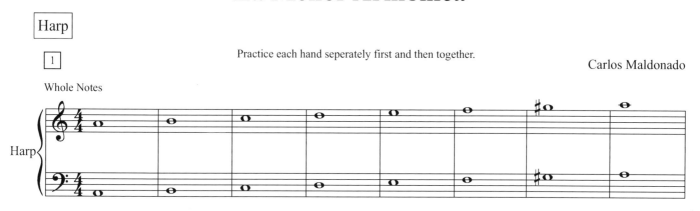

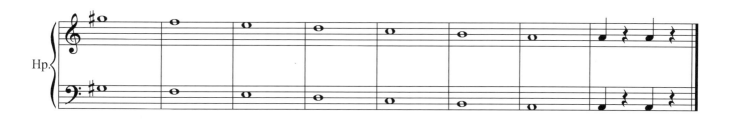

2

Half Notes

Whole Notes and Half Notes

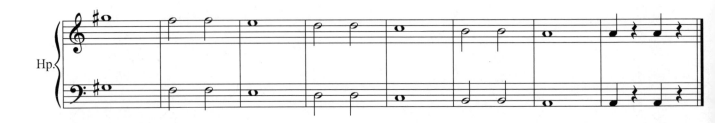

Half Note and Quarter Note

Half Note and Quarter Note

Quarter Notes

Eighth Notes

8

Quarter Notes and Eighth Notes 1

Quarter Notes and Eighth Notes 2

Quarter Notes and Eighth Notes 3

11

Quarter Notes and Eighth Notes 4

12

Quarter Notes and Eighth Notes 5

Quarter Notes and Quarter Rest 1

Quarter Notes and Quarter Rest 2

Quarter Notes, Eighth Notes and Rest

Sixteenth Notes

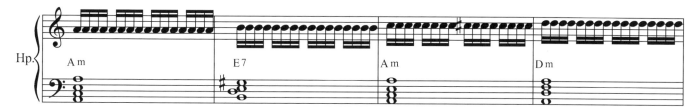

Sixteenth Notes and Eighth Notes

Sixteenth Notes and Quarter Notes

Tadimi

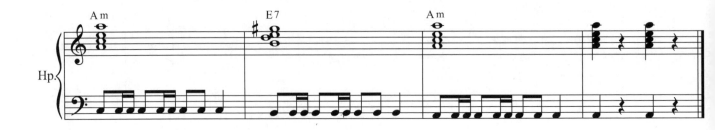

Takadi

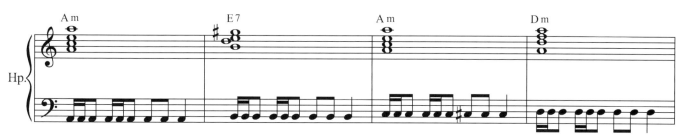

21

Dotted Half Note 1

22

Dotted Half Note 2

Dotted Quarter Note 1

24

Dotted Half Note 2

Dotted Eighth Note 1

26

Dotted Eighth Note 2

27

Syncopation 1

28

Syncopation 2

Quarter Note Triplet 1

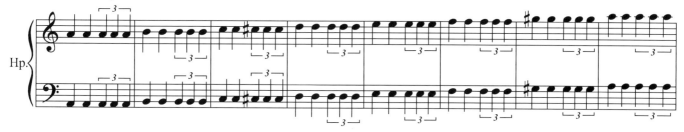

Quarter Note Triplet 2

Eighth Note Triplet

A Harmonic Minor In 3rds

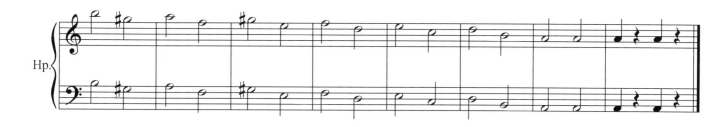

Quarter Note Scale Study

Half Note and Quarter Note Scale Study

Eighth Note and Quarter Note Scale Study

Dotted Quarter Note Scale Study

37

Dotted Half Note

38

Quarter Notes

Half Note and Quarter Note 1

40

Half Note and Quarter Note 2

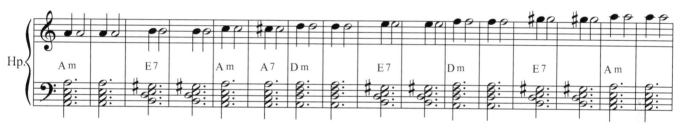

Quarter Notes and Eighth Notes 1

Quarter Notes and Eighth Notes 2

Quarter Notes and Eighth Notes 3

44

Eighth Notes

Dotted Quarter Note 1

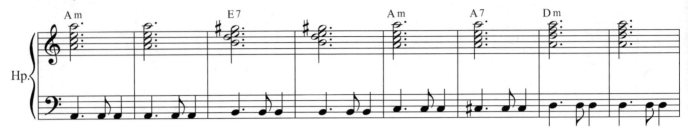

Dotted Quarter Note 2

Dotted Quarter Note 3

48

Syncopation 1

Syncopation 2

A Harmonic Minor In 3rds

Quarter Note Scale Study

Half Note and Quarter Note Scale Study

Eighth Note and Quarter Note Scale Study

54

Half Notes

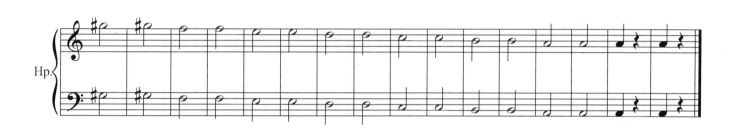

55

Half Note and Quarter Note 1

Half Note and Quarter Note 2

Eighth Notes

Quarter Notes and Eighth Notes 1

Quarter Notes and Eighth Notes 2

60

Quarter Notes and Eighth Notes 3

Quarter Notes and Eighth Notes 4

Quarter Notes and Eighth Notes 5

63

Quarter Notes and Quarter Rest 1

64

Quarter Notes and Quarter Rest 2

Quarter Notes, Eighth Notes and Rest

Sixteenth Notes and Eighth Notes

Tadimi

Takadi

Half Note and Quarter Note Tie 1

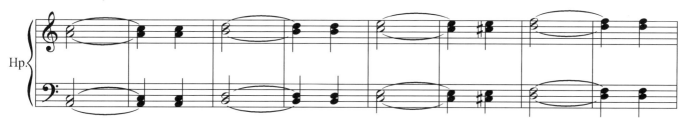

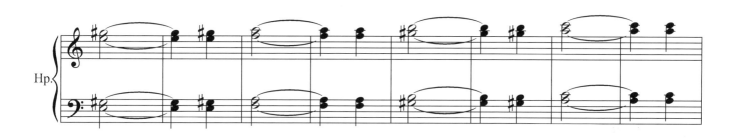

Half Note and Quarter Note Tie 2

Dotted Quarter Note 1

Dotted Quarter Note 2

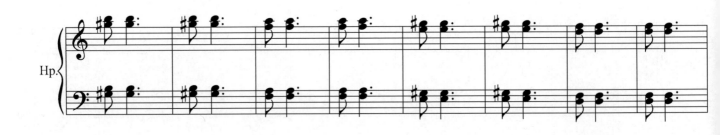

Dotted Eighth Note 1

75

Dotted Eighth Note 2

Syncopation 1

Syncopation 2

Quarter Note Triplet 1

Quarter Note Triplet 2

Eighth Note Triplet

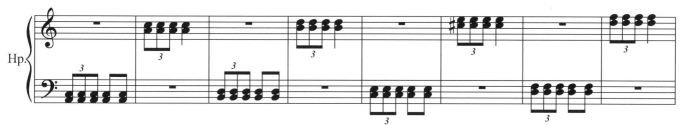

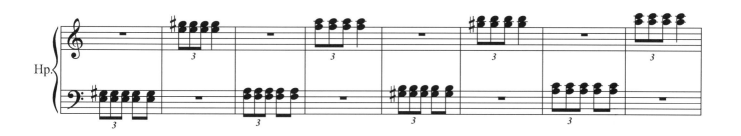

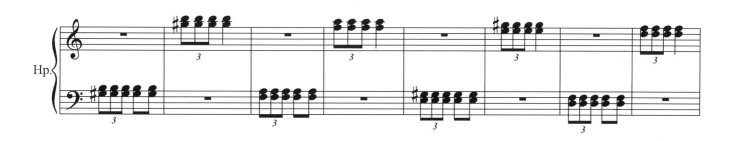

81

A Harmonic Minor In 3rds

82

Quarter Note Scale Study

83

Half Note and Quarter Note Scale Study

84

Eighth Note and Quarter Note Scale Study

Dotted Quarter Note Scale Study

Made in the USA
Columbia, SC
29 September 2024

43321984R00039